The Clothes Line:
The Amish of Ephrata

An Amish Novella on Morality

By
Sarah

Published by Price Publishing, LLC.
Morristown, New Jersey
2013

The Pennsylvania Dutch used in this manuscript is taken from the Pennsylvania Dutch Revised Dictionary (1991) by C. Richard Beam, Brookshire Publications, Inc. in Lancaster, PA.

Contact the author on Facebook at
http://www.facebook.com/fansofsarahprice or
visit her website at http://www.sarahpriceauthor.com

Price Publishing, LLC.
Morristown, NJ
http://www.pricepublishing.org

Other Books by Sarah Price

The Amish of Lancaster Series
#1: Fields of Corn
#2: Hills of Wheat
#3: Pastures of Faith
#4: Valley of Hope

The Amish of Ephrata Series
#1: The Tomato Patch
#2: The Quilting Bee
#3: The Hope Chest
#4: The Clothes Line

The Plain Fame Trilogy
Plain Fame
Plain Change
Plain Again

Serial Books
Amish Circle Letters Volume 1-10
Amish Circle Letters II Volume 1-10
Also released as Complete Novels

The Adventures of a Family Dog Series
#1: A Small Dog Named Peek-a-boo
#2: Peek-a-boo Runs Away
#3: Peek-a-boo's New Friends
#4: Peek-a-boo and Daisy Doodle

Other Books
Gypsy in Black
The Prayer Chain Series (with Ella Stewart)
Postcards from Abby (with Ella Stewart)
Meet Me in Heaven (with Ella Stewart)
Mark Miller's One: The Power of Faith
Cry of Freedom: Gettysburg's Chosen Sons
A Gift of Faith: An Amish Christmas Story
An Amish Christmas Carol: Amish Christian Classic Series
A Christmas Gift for Rebecca: An Amish Christian Romance

Find Sarah Price on Facebook and Goodreads!
Learn about upcoming books, sequels, series, and contests!

Foreword

Bullying is a serious problem. Too often, we read about cases of children bullying other children at school. It is, indeed, heartbreaking to read about the outcomes, quite often resulting in the victim committing suicide. Hindsight is twenty-twenty. We can point fingers at parents, schoolteachers, or even administrators for not doing more to stop the bullying and protect the innocent victims.

However, there is another form of bullying, a form that is not often discussed: adults bullying other adults.

Having been a victim myself, I learned the hard way that there are very few laws to protect *adults* from individuals who wish to continually bother us. Some states have strict laws, such as Florida, where cyber-bullying is punishable with jail time. Yet, despite having these laws, law enforcement personnel are, more often than not, unwilling to pursue such claims, leaving the victim to continue to receive harassing postings, emails, and private messages.

These laws must change.

The Internet provides too easy a forum for people to hide behind a keyboard and computer screen, communicating malicious messages with the intent to harm others. It's unchristian, unethical, and inhumane.

My challenge to everyone is to have an open dialogue about bullying and harassment using such tools as letters, emails, or postings on social media. If you recognize it, report it and block that person or remove yourself from that group. Supporting these individuals is supporting bullying. While turning the other cheek is a very noble concept, there comes a time when we have to find a way to help protect the victims from slander, harassment, and outright lies. After all, as the song goes, these bullies are "pretty good at lying".

S.P.

A Note About Vocabulary

The Amish speak Pennsylvania Dutch (also called Amish German or Amish Dutch). This is a verbal language with variations in spelling among communities throughout the USA. In some regions, a grandfather is "grossdaadi" while in other regions he is known as "grossdawdi".

In addition, there are words such a "mayhaps" or the use of the word "then" at the end of sentences and, my favorite, "for sure and certain" which are not necessarily from the Pennsylvania Dutch language/dialect but are unique to the Amish.

The use of these words comes from my own experience living among the Amish in Lancaster County, Pennsylvania.

Chapter One

The sun had risen over the back pasture and Priscilla paused at the kitchen window, a smile on her face as she stared outside, admiring the growing rows of pansies that she had just planted the previous weekend. In the distance, she saw some movement. At first, it was subtle, the hint of dark figures moving along the horizon where the hill dipped nonchalantly toward the road. But it didn't take long for her to realize that it was Stephen, already at work in his fields, plowing neat and even rows in the rich soil where he had spread fresh manure only a month ago.

Barely three weeks had passed since she had moved onto the farm. Despite having been married for five months, it had taken that long for Stephen to properly prepare the house for the arrival of his new bride. She hadn't minded the delay for he had visited her often at her parents' farm, stopping in for an early supper meal before returning to help his own daed with the evening chores. And, on the weekends, they had gone visiting members of both their families, a tradition among the Amish, and a time for their aunts and uncles and married siblings and cousins to gift them something special as a way of celebrating their nuptials.

Despite that, during the first months of their marriage, Priscilla had still felt as if they were merely courting. On the weekends, he would not stay with her at her parents' for he had too many chores to tend to at his own farm in the early morning hours. So, the day that Priscilla had moved to the farm had been the true start to their marriage, the day when she felt that she had become, indeed, Stephen's Priscilla.

She smiled to herself as she turned around, leaning against the counter and assessing her kitchen. The words rang in her ears and she loved the sound of it: *her* kitchen. It was large and roomy with a dividing wall at the far end. Beyond it was a large gathering room, one that would be used when church services would be held at their home. Since they had a larger farmhouse, they would host church services once or twice a year, depending on the rotation schedule that the bishop determined. While that room might hold the spiritual heart of the home, Priscilla knew that the physical and emotional heart of this home was its kitchen.

My kitchen, she thought as she hugged her arms to her chest and smiled to herself.

Yes, Stephen had done a wonderful *gut* job fixing up the house. He had put in new windows and hardwood floors as the original ones were all worn out. There were five small bedrooms upstairs that Priscilla hoped would one day be filled with their *kinner*. Their own bedroom was downstairs, a larger one with the doorway on the other side of the kitchen, near the staircase.

When Stephen had first brought her inside the house, it was the day after their wedding. They had spent their first night together as husband and wife at her parents' home. But they had both collapsed onto the bed, exhausted after having gotten up so early that morning and having stayed up so late. Stephen had wrapped his arms around her, holding her tight so that her back was pressed against his chest. She had fallen asleep feeling the gentle beat of his heart against her shoulder.

The following morning, they had helped her parents clean all of the remaining dishes, pots and pans before reorganizing the furniture on the first floor. Everything had been removed and stored in the barn in order to accommodate the large crowd of well-wishers that had gathered for the wedding service and the celebration that followed.

But afterwards, Stephen had lured her outside, holding her hand in his as he pulled her toward his awaiting buggy. She giggled as he stole a quick kiss, peeking around to make certain no one was spying on them, before helping her step inside.

"Today," he had told her. "I am taking you to our home. Now that we are married, no one will think twice if we are alone inside."

At their farm, Stephen had helped her out of the buggy and, after unharnessing the horse and setting him loose in the paddock adjacent to the barn, he had led her toward the front porch. For a moment, he had paused at the doorway, smiling at her. Then he had reached out with his hand and gently touched her cheek, a gesture of tenderness and love. She had blushed and lowered her eyes, all the while feeling her heart beat stronger and faster inside of her chest.

Once he had led her inside, he had turned around to watch her reaction. Indeed, Priscilla remembered her first thoughts as if that day had been just yesterday, not four months ago.

She had been amazed at the size of the kitchen and gathering room. Everything was large and open, bright and airy. There were enough windows to let in the natural light all day. The kitchen needed some work for the stove was clearly old and not functional. The counters were warped and a few of the cabinets had broken doors. But she saw the potential and, in her heart, knew that this was to become her home. Her own, real home.

"Oh Stephen," she had gasped. "It's just perfect!"

He had laughed at her. "Not yet, Priscilla, but soon. I promise."

He had taken her on a tour of the upstairs where there were several smaller bedrooms and one bathroom. Back downstairs, he had lingered by the door near the staircase and smiled at her. "I saved the best for last," he had murmured, his eyes staring at her as his hand reached for the doorknob.

Priscilla had flushed when he opened the door. Inside was the master bedroom and, unlike the other rooms, it was already fixed up with new flooring, fresh paint, and furniture. At the foot of the bed was her hope chest and lying atop the double bed was her quilt. Her beautiful wedding quilt, the one that she had made for Stephen the previous winter. He had watched her as she had walked into the room, noticing that everything was perfect and pristine in its presentation.

"Stephen," she had whispered, feeling emotion building in her throat. "I...I don't know what to say."

And, with that, he had shut the door and crossed the floor to take her into his arms, his embrace telling her how pleased he had been with her reaction. "Welcome home," he had whispered before he lowered his mouth to gently kiss her lips for the first time in their own home.

Priscilla felt the color rising to her cheeks at the memory. Not a day went by that she didn't thank the Lord for all that He had given to her. Stephen was truly the most *wunderbaar gut* man and she felt blessed each day that he had chosen her to be his wife; his Priscilla. Their days were filled with laughter and sunshine, even when the skies were grey and overcast with rainclouds.

During those first months of marriage, with the cold weather and shorter days, it had taken Stephen longer than he had anticipated fixing the downstairs of the house. But once it had been ready, he had been more than eager to bring home his bride.

At first, it had felt strange to wake up in a house that wasn't her parents'. She had lived her entire life at her parents' farm and had always been under the guidance and direction of her mamm. Mamm had set the schedule for baking bread, planting the garden and doing the laundry. Now, however, Priscilla had her own household to run and that meant having to make her own decisions.

Now, it was early April: time for planning her garden behind the house. Already Stephen had plowed and fertilized a patch of ground for her to plant all of the vegetables that she needed to can and preserve for winter. Luckily, during their weekend visits with family members, they had acquired enough gifts of ready made pickled beets, chow-chow, canned meat, and other necessities to carry them through until her garden would produce some of their own food.

Stephen had promised to take her to the market today to get her starter plants. She was looking forward to that time, just the two of them alone in the buggy, talking quietly as they drove down the winding back roads toward the store.

Despite living on their own farm, Stephen still insisted on stopping by his daed's farm once a day to help with early afternoon chores. Often, Priscilla would ride over there with him so that she could visit with his mamm and help her with baking or cooking. It was easy to tell that his parents were proud of the man they had raised. Indeed, Priscilla was just as proud to call him her husband.

"I see you are ready for a full afternoon of planting."

Priscilla turned around, surprised to see Stephen leaning against the doorway, watching her. "I hadn't heard you come in," she said, smiling as he approached her.

Placing his hands on her shoulders, he stared down into her face, his eyes soft and gentle as he searched hers. For a moment, she felt lost in his gaze, her heart swelling with love for this amazing, godly man that the Lord had blessed her with having as a husband.

"You realize," he said, his voice low and a twinkle in his eye. "This is the first of many gardens that we shall plant together, Priscilla."

The seriousness in his voice made her smile. "Ja, God willing," she replied.

"And I'm hoping you raise some of those famous, award winning tomatoes in this year's Esh garden," he finished.

At this statement, she laughed and felt the color rising to her cheeks. It had seemed so long ago that Stephen had outbid the bishop for her basket of tomatoes at the charity auction. That had truly been the start of their courtship and the moment that she had known that Stephen was the man for her.

He laughed with her and pulled her into his arms, embracing her for just a few short moments. Then, with a gentle kiss to the top of her head, the place where her parted hair peeked out from underneath her prayer kapp, he released her from his hold but still held her hand. "You ready then, my *fraa*?"

The horse was already harnessed to the buggy and Stephen helped her climb inside, the grey-topped black box wiggling as she settled into the plush velvet seat. When

Stephen climbed inside and sat beside her, he glanced at her and smiled. "Door open or closed?"

"Oh, open, I think," she said.

He nodded and left the door open so that, as the buggy rolled down the road, a light breeze could circulate the air inside. He also leaned forward and lifted the front window where the reins came inside. It snapped open to the top of the buggy roof. "Then let's go! Off to the garden center, *ja*?"

The drive down the back roads was peaceful and quiet. It was still early in the season so there were not many tourists, especially since today was a weekday. If there was one thing Priscilla dreaded, it was the summer season when the roads were clogged with cars filled with staring Englischers. Some of them liked to take photos, despite the Amish's opposition to the engraved image. During the summer, Priscilla always tried to avoid traveling to town on the weekends. It was best just to avoid the area, she always thought.

The garden center was a few miles away, located just outside of the town of Intercourse. The main traffic light was backlogged with cars and Stephen slowed down the horse so that the buggy could take its place in line.

Priscilla stared outside the open door and watched some of the people walking along the sidewalk by Zimmerman's Market. Most were Amish, but quite a few of the people were Englischers. She recognized one woman who lifted her hand and waved to Priscilla. She waved back with a smile and nudged Stephen to do the same.

They were passing another row of buildings when Priscilla caught her breath. "Stephen!" she gasped, her hand automatically reaching out to grab his arm. "Is that...?" She started to point but quickly remembered her manners.

"What is it?" Stephen glanced in the direction that Priscilla indicated.

Standing outside of a store was a familiar face: Susie Byler. With her blond hair and plump face, it was not hard to recognize her. However, Priscilla was startled by her disheveled appearance and apparent weight gain. And there was something sorrowful about her face, a lack of any expression whatsoever. *A truly lost soul,* Priscilla thought with a pang in her heart.

"Oh," he said under his breath. She noticed that he clenched his teeth, his jaw muscles tightening in his cheeks. "I guess that startled you, *ja*?"

Priscilla frowned and looked at him. "What do you mean? Startled me? I haven't seen her for quite a while and now I can barely recognize her!" She looked back out the window. "And what is she doing *there*?"

Stephen shrugged as the buggy rolled past the building. It was all Priscilla could do to not stare. Susie was sweeping the front walk of the building, her floral dress almost covering the thick, black sneakers that she wore on her feet. While her hair was pulled back in a bun, she wore neither prayer kapp nor head covering. It was clear that she had abandoned the Amish way of life.

"I didn't think to mention it to you," he said, his words forced and flat. "I had heard that she's been working there."

Again, Priscilla frowned. "At that tiny little gift shop?" That seemed like such an unlikely place for someone like Susie Byler to work. It was a small store, located off the main tourist track of Intercourse. There was also fierce competition from much larger gift stores right in the midst of the Kitchen Kettle Village. Certainly the store where Susie was working could not be very successful. Perhaps Stephen was mistaken, she wondered.

But, to Priscilla's surprise, Stephen nodded.

That news shocked Priscilla. She wasn't certain of what to say. It was a long distance for Susie to travel from her parents' farm, that was for sure and certain. And she couldn't imagine why Susie would be working at a gift store, especially since her parents needed the help on their farm. Hadn't it been Stephen who had stepped up to help Jacob Byler when he was ill, a few seasons back? Of course, that had backfired when Susie had tried to use his offer to help her daed to put a wedge between Priscilla and Stephen, claiming that Priscilla had stolen Stephen from her.

Now, how on earth did someone like Susie Byler know anything about working at a store? And an Englische gift store at that! Priscilla pondered.

"Oh help," Priscilla mumbled. "I don't think I dare ask anymore questions, Stephen. Best not to know." No, Susie Byler was not her favorite person, indeed. A troublemaker and a bully was all that this Susie Byler had turned out to be. And it had cost her plenty: the support of her church district and the respect of her community.

Stephen gave a soft laugh at his wife's reaction, clearly pleased that she did not want to speculate further about Susie and her fall from grace. "No, I don't think you do. Me neither. She's out of our lives finally and, from the looks of it, working harder now than ever before and probably for less reward." He shook his head, a dark cloud passing over his eyes. "And lost from God, it appears."

Priscilla shook her head, not wanting to think about that woman who had caused her and her family such angst. "Let's talk about something more pleasant, shall we? Like our garden!"

"Agreed!"

For the rest of the drive, Priscilla rattled off a list of the different plants that she considered for their vegetable garden: Beets and beans. Lettuce and peppers. Tomatoes and cucumbers. Stephen listened to her, nodding his head in approval at her selection of vegetables that, come early summer, would begin gracing their dinner table. His only suggestion was for a few watermelon plants and pumpkin vines to be added to her list.

The garden center was bustling with activity. Stephen hitched the horse to the metal railing before helping Priscilla climb down. "Seems we aren't the only ones with gardening on our mind," he said as he led her toward the entrance.

"Stephen Esh!"

Priscilla turned at the sound of her husband's name. She was surprised to see Steve Fischer, one of Stephen's friends who had just gotten married to Mimi Hostetler. She smiled and waited for Stephen to greet his friend.

"Picking up some plants for Mimi, ja?" he asked while shaking Steve's hand.

"Ja," Steve smiled, a sheepish look on his face.

Priscilla was surprised not to see his wife with him. "You be sure to tell Mimi that I said hello," she offered. "Haven't seen her since the wedding."

He nodded and put his hands into his front pockets,

rocking on his heels. "Been busy fixing up the house and all. But I'll be sure to tell her, Priscilla."

Priscilla left Stephen's side, letting him visit with his friend while she wandered through the different aisles, pulling a long flat wagon behind her so that she could load it with the plants that she wanted. She loved the smell of the young sprouts and held a tomato plant to her nose, inhaling deeply. Spring, she thought. It smelled like the best season of the year.

She set several flats onto the first rack of the cart: tomatoes, eggplants, beans, beets, lettuce, and herbs such as basil, parsley, and chives. She was arranging the trays when Stephen walked back over to join her. He peered over her shoulder to see what she had already collected.

"They look healthy, ja?"

She glanced at him and nodded. "Good selection this year, for sure and certain."

"You'll win some more awards, I reckon."

She laughed and gently tapped him on the shoulder. "Stephen!"

He laughed with her and helped push the cart further down the aisle. "Listen, Priscilla," he said, changing the subject. "Steve invited us over for an afternoon picnic on our next off Sunday. I told him we would visit."

"That sounds lovely!" Priscilla replied, pausing by the cucumber plants to select several to put onto the cart. "I'll have to bring a pie, I reckon."

It was strange that, now that they were married, their Sundays were not spent with other youths at singings or volleyball games. Those activities were for the unmarried members of their community. Now, as a newly married couple, their free time consisted of visiting other people, usually family. It would be nice indeed to visit with another young, newly married couple for a change.

They were on their way back home from the garden center when Stephen made one last stop along the back roads at another Amish farm. Priscilla looked at him, wondering why he was stopping. It was a farm she was not familiar with but there was a sign for hardware. He smiled at her, a twinkle in his eye as he gestured for her to stay put when he stopped the buggy at the hitching rail.

"I'll be just a quick moment," he said as he climbed out.

She leaned against the window, gazing into the blue sky. Several birds soared high above and she watched them, amazed at their grace, so perfect and regal. *Truly one of God's most amazing creatures,* she thought as she wondered what the world looked like from up there. Near the side of the store building on the farm stood a tall Purple Martin birdhouse. Two of the birds flew into different compartments, one with a piece of hay in its mouth. She smiled, realizing that it must be a mother bird preparing a nest for her eggs.

"What are you watching with such a lovely smile?" Stephen asked as he opened the back of the buggy and set a package inside on the floor, careful to not crush the plants.

Pointing toward the birdhouse, Priscilla explained what she had seen. "She must be nesting."

She saw him catch his breath, his eyes searching first for the birdhouse and then searching hers. "Spring is a right gut time to think about families, ja?" he said, his eyes boring into hers. "Mayhaps soon...?"

Priscilla flushed and averted her eyes.

Laughing at her modesty, Stephen reached out and touched her knee. "Later, I reckon," he said. "For now, we have a full day's work cut out for us. Planting your garden and hanging up your new clothes line!"

"My what?"

He backed up the buggy, tugging gently at the right rein so that the horse moved the buggy backward in that direction. When the buggy was clear of the hitching rail, Stephen urged the horse forward. "Your clothes line! I just bought you a new wheel to hang."

"What was wrong with my old one?"

He shrugged. "Hoping that you'll need a bigger one soon," he teased, nudging her with his arm. "That small one just won't do when we have lots of kinner!"

She blushed again and looked out the window, secretly pleased with Stephen's desire for a large family. She, too, prayed that she would be able to provide him with plenty of sons to help with the farm work and daughters to help her with her own chores.

Her eyes lingered on the birdhouse as the buggy drove by. The bird sat on the edge of the opening, chirping into the gentle breeze before lifting itself in flight to find more hay or grass to complete the nest inside. A mother's instinct, she thought, watching the birdhouse grow smaller as the buggy moved further away. She smiled to herself and nestled back against the seat, her shoulder brushing against Stephen's as she wondered how soon she would feel the urge to start her own nesting.

Chapter Two

It was Saturday. The sun was shining and a gentle breeze blew through the open windows in the kitchen. The trees were just starting to show green from the buds of spring leaves. Priscilla stood at the window and stared outside, her eyes on the far field where Stephen was working. Four large cream-colored Belgian draft horses pulled the grass cutter. It was not the usual time for a hay cutting but the winter had been light and the spring had come earlier than usual.

She could see the new clothes line, hanging from the corner of the house. It stretched across the driveway all the way to the upper point of the barn roofline. True to his word, Stephen had hung it the very same day that he had bought it. Priscilla had watched from the ground, holding her breath, when he had climbed atop the barn roof. He looked far too high in the air for her liking. But he had only laughed at her apprehension, pausing to wave before he leaned over the edge to hang the new wheel.

Today, however, was the first day that she had used it. After the breakfast dishes had been cleaned, she had tackled the laundry. Unlike at her mamm's house, Priscilla only had to do laundry twice a week. With just two people living at the farm, there wasn't much laundry to require more of her attention. But today, she was especially pleased to look out the window and see the bedding and towels hanging from the line near the barn roof while Stephen's pants and shirts hung closer to the house. In the middle were her colorful dresses. This clothes line was, indeed, longer than the old one and she could hang all of their laundry at once, and with space to spare.

She had always loved looking at the colorful clothes hanging from the lines at neighbors' farms. It was as if each one told a story about the families. Priscilla liked to play a guessing game on trips to town, trying to figure out how many people lived on the farms based upon the clothes lines. Five flat sheets certainly meant at least four kinner plus the parents. Multiple dresses in different sizes hinted that the mother had *dochders*. Tiny black pants, hanging by just the straps of very small suspenders, told the story of a future farmer growing up in that particular house.

It had often dawned on Priscilla that, despite being so private about their emotions and their lifestyle, the Amish certainly told a very public story when they hung their clothes out to dry for anyone to see and analyze.

Of course, she also knew that the Amish women, particularly the older Amish women, played other games with their clothes lines. They liked to talk amongst themselves about who managed to hang out their clean clothes first in the morning.

Many Amish women stuck to the traditional schedule of wash on Mondays. That way, the Sunday clothes didn't have to wait to be washed. Some women awoke extra early and did the laundry before breakfast so that it was already hanging on the line well before the sun crested the horizon. It was a moment of unspoken pride to be the first to have the family clothes flapping in the breeze, ready to soak in the bright sunrays and the fresh morning scents.

And, of course, there was also the color game. Priscilla smiled to herself, vowing that she would never get caught into that prideful game of who could make their clothesline look the prettiest. Black pants would hang together then black dresses and aprons then the burgundy dresses, blue dresses, green dresses, and pink dresses. Dark colors would be grouped together and pastels at the end closest to the house. It was a way to be creative and fun while tackling a taxing chore.

But there was also another game: a game of deceit and lies. There were some women who would get up early and hang out dirty clothes just so that they could be the first one on their lane to have a rainbow colored line of clothes fluttering in the wind. It didn't really fool anyone, not after a while. Especially when the children showed up for school or at church in less than pristine outfits. It spoke more of the prideful and lying character of the woman than anything else.

Pride and lies, Priscilla thought. Over a silly clothes line! Two very bad sins that were frowned upon by the people, regardless of which church district they lived in.

Turning away from the window, Priscilla glanced around the room. Everything looked in perfect order and that was right important to Priscilla on this day, for some of her friends were coming to visit and share the noon meal with her. Stephen had agreed, knowing that it wasn't easy for Priscilla to suddenly be on a farm alone, without anyone to talk to, while he worked in the barn and fields. She enjoyed helping him with the morning and evening milking, but, other than those few hours and mealtime, she was alone during the better part of the day.

Sarah and Polly arrived shortly before eleven o'clock, surprising Priscilla even more as they brought along Polly's cousin, Sylvia. She had returned from Ohio to spend the spring with her extended family in Ephrata, Pennsylvania.

They all carried cardboard boxes full of canned food

with them, more contributions to the pantry of the newly married Esh's. Priscilla fussed over their generous gifts and set everything onto the counter. There were canned beets, applesauce, chow-chow, and even canned meat. It was more than enough to carry her through until her own garden began to flourish.

"I don't know what to say," she gushed.

Polly laughed. "Always so modest, Priscilla...Esh!"

The women laughed at Polly's emphasis on her new last name. Even Priscilla joined in, blushing modestly before gesturing to the table for her friends to sit.

Sarah was the first to move over to the table and sit down. "Tell us everything! How does it feel to have your own home?"

While Sylvia and Polly joined Sarah at the sturdy farmer's table, Priscilla hurried to the propane-operated refrigerator where she had left a pitcher of fresh meadow tea to cool. When she carried it to the table, she set it in the center. "Oh it's different," she admitted. "I'm so thankful that my mamm taught me so much. Without having her around to tell me what to do, I have to make my own schedule. It's not as easy as I thought."

"Meadow tea?" Sarah said, her eyes sparkling at the taste of the drink. "Now, where did you get that one from? Ours hasn't even begun to sprout in the garden just yet!"

"Mamm had frozen some concentrate last fall," Priscilla admitted. "I just love meadow tea. So refreshing, ja?"

It was after the meal was finished and the dishes cleaned that the four women retreated outside to sit at the picnic table that Stephen had set up under the large oak tree near the driveway. It was cool in the shade and a perfect afternoon for visiting. Sylvia and Sarah had their heads bent over linens that they were cross-stitching while Polly and Priscilla crocheted doilies that they would sell at the local Amish stores.

That was when the conversation turned to the local news.

"I heard that Susie Byler moved away from her parents," Sarah mentioned. "She's working at a store in Intercourse."

Priscilla gasped. "Moved away? I wondered that!" She glanced at her friends. "Although, I just saw her working in Intercourse the other day when Stephen and I went to the garden center! At that small gift store near Kitchen Kettle, I reckon."

Sylvia remained unusually silent while Sarah nodded her head. "Ja, I heard that, too."

"Why on earth would she have moved out from her parents' house?"

Polly gave a typical *tsk, tsk* in response. "Seems her mamm's been going back to the bottle a bit. Evil in that."

Sarah raised an eyebrow. "I heard it is more than a little bit."

"Really?" This news was shocking to Priscilla. After all, alcohol use was not typical but certainly not unheard of among the Amish. And the Byler parents were baptized members of the church. But if Susie's mamm was *back* into drinking, she would be shunned, for sure and certain. Just one more unfortunate hardship for the Byler family.

Sarah nodded, a solemn expression on her face. "Oh ja," she added. "And a nasty spell she's going through. Taking quite a bit out on that daughter of hers for getting them shunned."

Priscilla looked up, startled by Sarah's words. "But they weren't shunned."

With a casual shrug of the shoulder, Sarah seemed to indicate otherwise. "Told to move church districts might just feel like being shunned, ain't so? And I heard from my brother that this drinking business is quite the issue for their new *g'may*. The bishop isn't used to alcoholics among the adults. One of the reasons Susie moved out and took that job."

Priscilla frowned. She didn't like gossip and certainly not about that particular woman. She had heard more than enough and hoped to change the direction of the conversation. "I don't think I want to ruin the day talking about that Susie. She's not been bothering me since the bishop sent her away."

"Lucky you," Sylvia added glumly. The downcast look in her eyes made it clear that there was more to the story than met the eye. The other women looked up, staring at Sylvia as they tried to ascertain what she had meant by her comment. The sad expression on her face made it clear that something was bothering her.

"Is everything alright, Sylvia?" Priscilla asked.

There was a hesitation, a moment of withdrawal before Sylvia finally shook her head. "Nee," was all she said.

"What is it, then?"

Polly rolled her eyes as she set down her crocheting. "Not again, Sylvia. Please tell me you haven't received another one!"

Priscilla looked at her friends, confused by the conversation. Certainly she was missing something for she did not understand what they were talking about. "Another one what?"

"Letters," Sarah answered for Sylvia, a serious look on her face. "She's been receiving horrid letters from an anonymous person."

"I don't believe you!" Priscilla gasped, staring first at Sarah and then Sylvia.

"Well, not always anonymous," Sylvia added with a sigh. "The first few had *your* return address on them."

At this news, Priscilla felt the color drain from her face. Could it be possible that Susie Byler had shifted her attention to someone else to bully? Yet, at the same time, she was busy impersonating her original target! Priscilla felt her heart begin to beat faster as she wondered at the depths to this woman's misery. "What do you mean? They had *my* return address?"

"Ja," Sylvia said, lifting her eyes to stare at Priscilla. "I hadn't wanted to tell you. But they keep coming and are signed with your name. They even have this address as the sender."

"But certainly not written by my hand!" Priscilla stared at the other women. She was stunned by this announcement and horrified that anyone would think she could write letters that were anything but godly and Christian. "You know that, don't you?"

Sarah reached over and touched Priscilla's hand. "Of course, we all do," she replied. "You are not capable of writing such vile and horrid things. Polly and I received letters too, just before Sylvia received hers. Letters that said you are no true Christian and not to be believed."

"Me?"

Both Sarah and Polly nodded their heads at the same time.

Priscilla felt her heart race. "And were those letters signed?"

"Nee," Polly admitted. "Not by name."

"'An Amish Friend'," Sarah said. "That's what mine was signed."

Priscilla could scarcely believe her ears. It was incredulous to her that Susie hadn't stopped her crazy antics yet. Surely she was a mad woman, intent on trying to ruin lives. "I don't even know what to say," she whispered. "It doesn't sound like it could be true!" She looked at Polly. "You don't know for sure and certain that it's Susie, though."

"Nee, we don't," Polly admitted with a sigh. "But who else would do such a thing?" She reached into her pocket and withdrew a folded piece of paper. "Mayhaps you'd like to read this?" She slid it across the table toward Priscilla who merely stared at it for a moment, as if a true serpent had been placed right in front of her on the picnic table. "Go on, read it."

Reluctantly, Priscilla reached for the piece of paper. Her fingers hesitated over it and she glanced at the three women seated before her. Polly nodded encouragement while Sylvia kept her eyes downcast. Picking up the letter, Priscilla unfolded it, the paper crinkling in the silence, and read through the words, her heart beginning to palpitate and her stomach lurching as if she might be getting sick:

I am a friend who believes you need to know the truth about what kind of person you have been associating with. I have enclosed evidence against Priscilla Smucker/Esh! I hope you will see how much you have been lied to by Priscilla Smucker, and who was telling you the truth all along!

Signed,

An Amish Friend

Stunned, Priscilla looked up. She could hardly believe the words that she had just read. It didn't seem real. Could this really be happening *again*? "Lied about what? And what is this 'evidence' that she's talking about?"

"Look at the second page."

Indeed, on the second page was a document, a legal-looking document, stamped with a round seal that said Lancaster County. As Priscilla's eyes tried to make sense of it, her heart began to pound, her head felt dizzy, and she feared that she might faint. Indeed, despite knowing nothing of the Englische legal system, it certainly looked as some official document showing that the police had been involved. "Is this...?"

"It appears to be what they call a restraining order. States that you and Stephen went to her new house on February 5th and threatened her."

At this, Priscilla flung the paper across the table. Her cheeks burned red and she felt tears brimming at the corners of her eyes. "Get that evil accusation away from me!"

Sarah reached out to touch Priscilla's hand, comforting her while Polly shook her head and picked up the papers. "Oh please, Priscilla! It's not real. I had my brother, Gid, ask his friend about it, you know that Mennonite that he hangs out with. He knows Englische law better than us."

"Oh help," Priscilla muttered again, waving her hand

before her face, fighting the tears that threatened to fall down her cheeks. "I have to talk to Stephen about this." She glanced behind her at the calendar hanging on the wall. "And February 5th was a weekend! We were visiting with family." Even from where she sat, she could still see the dates circled when they had gone visiting during their first months of marriage. She had brought the calendar with her from her parents' home and had hung it in the kitchen. "In fact, on that day, we were with his cousins in Lititz, just down the road."

The other women nodded.

"We know that," Sarah said.

"Besides," Priscilla continued, her tears suddenly dissipating as her hurt began to turn to anger. "I don't even know where she lives now! And I have plenty more to do than to bother with the likes of her and her craziness."

"A trailer park just south of Intercourse is what I heard," Sarah added.

That announcement caused Priscilla to stop in midsentence. "A what?"

"Trailer park. She's living in one of those Englische houses that are pulled by cars." Sarah pointed toward the paper that Polly was folding up in order to slide it back into the envelope. "States in this so-called restraining order that you shall not trespass at the Country Haven Campground where she is staying, nor approach her trailer."

"And she filed this...this restraining order against me? And the police believed her just like that?" The entire situation sounded incredulous to Priscilla. What crazy laws the Englische have, she thought.

Polly rolled her eyes. "She's pretty good at lying."

Priscilla was speechless. Lying? That was an understatement. How was it possible that someone who had professed to walk with Christ could make up such stories and be able to live with herself afterwards?

Polly tried to reassure her again. "Listen to Sarah. Gid's friend found out that anyone can file for something like this and even have it stamped but, unless a police officer brings it to you, it's not legal. Obviously the judge didn't sign anything nor did he believe her."

Regardless, Priscilla was in shock. First Susie had taken out that ad in The Budget, telling everyone those horrible lies about her and Stephen. Now, she was mailing horrid letters to her friends and filing false documents with law officials! What exactly was Susie trying to prove? What was her motivation? Her motive? Would her personal vendetta ever end? Priscilla just didn't understand what fueled her anger.

Indeed, this was not good news at all. Everything had been so quiet, so calm. Why would Susie Byler continue her harassment and now, to spread the cloak to her friends? "I simply don't understand this woman," Priscilla muttered, a growing pit in her stomach. "I feel that we should pray for her, pray for the return of her mental health which, clearly, she no longer has."

Polly and Sarah scoffed while Sylvia grew more despondent. "I won't be praying for that lost soul," Sarah added, not too kindly. "She's done more than enough to harm you and now us. But any letters that come for me, I just throw them in the rubbish heap. After all, that's where they belong."

It was later that evening when Priscilla finally had a chance to talk to Stephen about what she had learned from her friends. She repeated the story to her husband who, to her surprise, said nothing. But his expression spoke of his disapproval in what she told him. With his lips pressed tightly together, he continued with his chores, Priscilla working alongside of him.

"Have you nothing to say, Stephen?" she found the courage to ask, fearful that she had upset him by sharing the story.

"Nee," Stephen replied tersely. Despite what he said, she could tell that he was upset. "I do not."

Priscilla fought the sinking feeling inside of her stomach. Surely he was unhappy with her for what he must consider idle gossip. Without another word, Priscilla bent her head to the side of the cow that she was milking, trying to focus her attention on the task at hand and not at her beating heart. Had she upset him? Was sharing that story truly gossip? It worried her that he might feel that she was just that: a gossiper.

Several minutes passed before she heard him mutter something under his breath and, when she looked up, she was surprised to see him reach for his hat and rip it from atop his head. He stood up and began to pace in the aisle behind the cows, shaking his head and mumbling to himself; she couldn't exactly hear what he was saying.

"Stephen?"

He exhaled loudly and turned to stare at his young wife.

His eyes looked as though they were on fire, an expression Priscilla had never seen on his face before. "When will it stop?" he said, none too kindly. "First it was jealousy over the tomatoes. Then it was trying to break us apart and turn the community against you over the wedding quilt. When that did not work, she tried to make both of us look as though we were unchristian with that horrible letter to the Budget!" He raised his clenched fist into the air. "When will it stop? Tell me that, Priscilla! When?"

Without a second's hesitation, Priscilla jumped up from the stool she had been seated upon by the cow and ran to her husband. Placing her hands on his arms, she tried to calm him down. "Don't let her win, Stephen. Please," she pleaded. "We are so much stronger than she is and we have the love and support of not just each other but the entire community." She tried to force a weak smile. "She has nothing, ain't so? No family, no real friends, no true faith in God."

Her words seemed to soften his fierce expression and look of determination.

"Stephen," she continued, trying to calm down her husband's anger. "You are such a godly man, so pure in thought and action. Don't let someone like Susie Byler change that. Not for one second, you hear?"

"Ja, I hear you, *fraa*," he said, his tone softening as he listened to her words. Yet, she could tell that he was still distressed. "It just sickens me to think that she actually believes that she has fooled anyone. And it pains me to harbor such ill thoughts against one who clearly is in need of prayers more than most."

Priscilla held his hands and smiled, a real smile this

36

time, not forced. "I would expect nothing less from you, Stephen Esh: to recognize that she is a woman in pain and in great need of prayer. Mayhaps we should pray for her salvation together...right now?"

He hesitated, staring down at his wife and pondering her words. She could sense his inner conflict and knew that her Stephen would come to the proper conclusion. And that, he did. With a sigh, he took his wife's hand and led her toward the back of the barn so that they could kneel by the hay bales. With their heads bowed down and their hands clasped before them, they both said a silent prayer to God, praying for His eternal love to shine on all of them, especially Susie Byler who needed His love and compassion more than most.

Chapter Three

It was at the following church service when Priscilla noticed that Sylvia was not well. She looked thin, too thin, and there were dark circles under her eyes. However, since Priscilla now sat with the married Amish women, she knew she wouldn't be able to find out what was bothering her friend until it was time for the fellowship meal.

From across the room, her eyes continued to glance in Stephen's direction. The young growth of his beard clearly identified him as a newly married man and, the way that his eyes drifted toward her time and again made it clear who his bride was.

After the second sermon by the bishop, the Ausbund books were opened to Song 91 for the closing hymn of the service. Priscilla reached beneath the wooden bench where she sat to pick up the chunky Ausbund book and opened it to page 475 where the song began:

> O child of man, understand me now,
> I want to give you a summary
> Of how one should fear the Lord,
> And live according to His will.
> In the fear of the Lord, you shall be pure,
> Which He allows to flow through you
> Here in this time.
> It will bring you wisdom,
> Perception and true righteousness,
> So that you can shun evil.
>
> The fear of God is a beginning
> Of wisdom that is pure.

It produces repentance
In this time of opportunity.
Wisdom alone acknowledges
What is genuine righteousness.
It makes a distinction here,
In a life of godliness,
Herein the Holy Spirit gives confirmation,
Whereby one is called sanctified in this time,
To the one to whom God gives this gift.

This fear also raises questions here,
Of unfamiliar things.
If you are given a discernment,
Then take it deeply to heart.
Take wisdom with you as your counsel,
Consider what the issues of life and death are,
Until it makes them plain to you.
Then the distinction will be made,
When wisdom gives you the clear discernment,
It will divide life from death.

Faith comes from this understanding,
Thereto also love.
These gifts flow forth from God alone,
Faith and love live in hope.
We are assured of these here.
All that God has promised
Shall be appropriated by patience.
If you have faith, love, hope and patience,
You are truly standing in God's mercy,
And experience His glory.[1]

Priscilla lost herself in the words that were being sung, listening to each drawn out syllable and feeling the power of each word. The congregation waited for the first syllable of

---

[1] Ausbund Song 91, Verse 1-4.

each line to be sung by Yonie Esh, Stephen's cousin, before joining in, singing the rest of the verse.

When the congregation sang the last verse, Priscilla paused at the words: *faith, love, hope* and *patience.* She wanted so much to stand in God's mercy but had been guilty of judging others and lacking love for her fellow neighbor. A wave of guilt washed over her and she realized that she needed to focus more on forgiveness, even when her patience was stretched too thin. In order to be a true servant of God, she needed to focus more on her fear of God, not her fear of mankind.

When the congregation stood up and turned to face the outer walls of the building, before kneeling in a final prayer, Priscilla felt refreshed and eager to face the rest of the day. She knew what she had to do: recognize true righteousness and practice patience when it came to things that caused her stress. She said a silent prayer, asking God for the strength to do His will in a stronger manner.

After the service, the men began to convert the wooden benches into long tables by slipping the bench legs into wooden boards. While the men worked, the younger boys scurried around the room, collecting the Ausbund books to store in a wooden crate. The women, however, began to prepare the meal for fellowship. Even the younger girls helped by carrying plates and utensils to the tables, setting them for the first seating that was about to start.

Priscilla busied herself, carrying plates of cold cuts and bread to the tables, smiling at the other women who were helping. Despite what appeared to be chaos, with men and women scurrying about the room, it was completely organized. Everyone knew what work needed to be done.

Men sat at the first table and women at the second. There was a long moment of silence as the bishop bowed his head, the others following his example. Those who were not eating during the first seating stood along the wall and lowered their head as they joined the silent prayer. Only when the bishop made a movement with his hand did the others begin to reach for the plates of food to serve themselves.

The older members of the congregation and the mothers with younger children always ate first. The single women and the women without any children would replenish their drinks while they waited for their turn. Priscilla found a moment to stand with Polly and Sarah during a break in the work.

"Sylvia doesn't look well," Priscilla managed to whisper to Polly after the first seating of people began to eat. "Is she alright then?"

Polly shook her head. "Mamm had her go to the doctor. He has her on special medicine for her blood pressure. Seems it's too high."

"Is that so?" Priscilla asked, concern in her eyes. Sylvia was too young to be suffering from high blood pressure. And, since she was visiting her cousin, not feeling well was certainly an even stronger inconvenience. "Whatever could cause that?"

"Stress," Polly answered, leveling her gaze at Priscilla. There was something strong and determined in Polly's eyes. "The letters keep coming. And now she won't show them to us. They are apparently too vile to even let others read."

Letters? Priscilla could scarce believe it. While she was relieved that Susie had stopped bothering her, it disturbed her that Sylvia had now become the prime target. Yet, she remembered her prayer, to practice being more patient and godly. Rather than merely spend time talking about Susie, it was time to get others involved. "I think she needs to go to the bishop, to tell him what is happening," Priscilla said firmly. "He'll know what to do. Such matters are best handled by him, I reckon."

Polly shrugged her shoulders. "What *can* he do? If it is Susie Byler, she's no longer part of our district and, from what I heard, she's getting herself mixed up in Englische things that are probably making matters worse."

That caught Priscilla's attention. Despite being in the same *g'may* as before she was married, Stephen's farm was at the further edge of their church district. With so much to be done on the farm, she hadn't had much time for visiting since her friends had stopped by, the week before. "What types of Englische things?" she asked suspiciously.

"Well, you know that her mamm was caught with the bottle by their new *g'may*. Some speculate that Susie is following down the same path."

"Oh help!" Priscilla said, pressing her hand against her chest. The evils of alcohol were something she had only heard about but never experienced, thankfully. It was rare to hear about Amish who drank, and certainly not after baptism. To drink as a baptized member of the church meant risking to be shunned. But, then again, Susie had been denied her baptism.

Sarah leaned forward. "Heard it's more than speculation about that girl and alcohol. Seems to get worse at night, making calls on the telephone to people and leaving horrid messages."

"I don't believe you!" Priscilla gasped. "This is just more gossip, ain't so?"

Sarah shook her head before she continued. "Calling and leaving messages at different farms on the community phones. Everyone says she's just plain ole nuts and the booze is making her worse. Downright nasty and mean, that's Susie Byler."

"Stop, please!" Priscilla put her hands to her ears as if to shield herself from more unpleasant news. "I can't bear to hear more!"

"Just be glad that she's leaving *you* alone for now," Polly added as she reached for the pitcher of water and walked to the table to refill everyone's glasses.

"No," Priscilla said, more to herself than to Sarah. "I will pray for her, instead. That's what God would want: prayer for that woman and for our friend, Sylvia."

"Prayer won't help that woman, I fear," Sarah quipped before she, too, hurried to see if anyone needed to have his or her drink replenished.

Wandering into the kitchen, Priscilla tried to busy herself by helping the older women. She wanted to distance herself from the latest news about Susie. She was, indeed, quite glad that Stephen did not have a phone on the property. One less thing to worry about. If someone needed to reach them, they would have to stop by the farm, mail a letter through the postal service, or contact them via the shared community farm on the main lane.

One of the older women smiled at Priscilla as she picked up a towel and began to dry dishes by the sink. That was one of the things that Priscilla enjoyed the most about church Sunday: the camaraderie of the women as they cleaned up between meals. She had never minded the work of washing dishes for over two hundred people. With so many women helping, it hardly felt like work. But she enjoyed hearing the latest news from her neighbors, both near and far.

Stephen's farm was one of the farther ones in the district and, as such, far away from many of the other farms. It had only been by chance that his farm had not been included in the redistricting several years ago. Since no one had lived at Stephen's farm and it was adjacent to his daed's, the bishop had extended the border of the new district just beyond the farm. Priscilla would always be grateful for that decision for, without it, he might have attended other singings and found himself taking home another Amish girl instead of her.

"How's the new farm, then?" the older woman asked Priscilla.

"Right *gut, danke*," she replied, setting the dry dish on the counter. "We just planted our first garden last week. The soil sure looks dark and rich so I'm hopeful that we have some success."

The woman laughed, the deep lines of her face telling the unspoken story of many years of gardening in the sun. "Of that I'm sure," she said and patted Priscilla's arm. "You always had that green thumb, ja?"

"No more so than anyone else, I reckon," Priscilla replied modestly.

The woman smiled at Priscilla's comment. "Time will tell on that one." There was a knowing look in the woman's eyes and Priscilla felt herself flush at the unspoken compliment. Her gardening skills were renown in the community, despite her best efforts to downplay the extra attention.

It was just a few minutes later when Priscilla felt a tug

at her sleeve and, setting down the dishtowel she had in her hand, she turned to see who was trying to catch her attention. It was Sylvia, her face pale and drawn. She truly looked ill and Priscilla set the towel down on the counter.

"Why Sylvia!" she exclaimed. "What has happened? Shall I fetch you some water?"

In response, Sylvia shook her head but motioned Priscilla to the side, signaling that she wanted to speak to her in private. Together, they walked to the back of the large room and slipped through a door onto the back screened in porch. It was a warm day and, in the distance, children were scampering about, playing with each other in the side yard. Otherwise, they were alone.

"I received a new letter," Sylvia whispered, slipping a folded sheet of paper into Priscilla's hand. "I want you to read it."

Priscilla hesitated, not wanting to read another one of those letters. "I don't think I want to, Sylvia."

But Sylvia insisted. There was something sorrowful about Sylvia's eyes that caught Priscilla's attention: A look of pleading for her understanding. With a sigh, she took the paper from her friend and, with a quick glance over her shoulder to make certain no one could see, Priscilla unfolded it.

Sylvia,

You are not the person we thought you to be. Your faith is not genuine. A true Christian would not be fake.

Priscilla S.

It took a moment for the words to sink in. And then, when the enormity of the message hit her, Priscilla's eyes grew wide and she immediately looked at Sylvia. "You know that I didn't write that!" she whispered, shoving the paper back at Sylvia.

"Of course I know that, Priscilla," Sylvia replied, a touch of irritation in her voice. "You are not capable of thinking such evil thoughts. Do you think we are so foolish as to believe you would write something so vile? She may think we are stupid but I can assure you that it just ain't so!"

A shiver ran up Priscilla's spine and she shuddered. To question Sylvia's faith was unthinkable! Besides playing the role of God by judging Sylvia's faith, it was also one of the most insulting things a person could say. *Judge not, that ye be judged not,* Priscilla thought. Immediately, she felt her own anger start to swell, especially given the fact that whoever had written this had tried to impersonate her!

"I need to go step outside for a spell," she said, her voice hoarse and her hands trembling.

Before she could turn away, she felt a hand on her arm. "Priscilla!" Sylvia said. "You promise me that you won't tell a soul!"

Promise? How could Priscilla make such a promise? It wasn't even a fair question. "Sylvia," she said. "I would never make a promise that I cannot keep. And that is one that I cannot make, my friend. She is trying to make me look like a horrible person. Again. You need to involve the bishop. Let him handle this for once and for all."

"I shouldn't have told you," Sylvia mumbled, her eyes downcast as she refolded the paper.

A momentary wave of guilt washed over Priscilla. Her friend was clearly distressed, understandably so. If anyone questioned her own faith or called her a fake Christian, Priscilla would not know how to respond. It would crush her spirit and cause her to doubt her own beliefs. The thought dawned on her that crushing Sylvia's spirit was exactly the intent of the writer of that note. Clearly, Sylvia had told her about the note for a reason and that reason was most likely to ask for her support.

Reaching out, Priscilla clutched Sylvia's hand. "I'm ever so sorry," she said. "I will make that promise, Sylvia. This is not about me but about you. I won't tell anyone, if that is what you truly wish. I reckon it's like keeping someone else's dirty laundry off the clothes line, ain't so? No need to put it out there for everyone to see."

Something softened in Sylvia's eyes. *"Danke,"* she whispered. "I thought you should know since she's bringing your name into this."

"You do know none of that is true, Sylvia? You are not a fake Christian." Priscilla coaxed, hoping her words would give her friend strength. "You know that, ja?"

Sylvia nodded but there was doubt in her expression.

"Sylvia, if that is, indeed, Susie Byler, it certainly tells more about her than anything else. A person with a pure and truly faithful heart could never write such a horrid note. She is simply filled with malice." Priscilla took a deep breath and released Sylvia's hand. "We should all feel sorry for her, I reckon. Pray for her healing."

"I won't be praying for that woman!" Sylvia snapped, her eyes suddenly fierce and full of venom. "She's too evil for prayers. Not from me, anyway."

Priscilla wanted to argue with Sylvia and to remind her that Jesus came to provide salvation for the sinners, not just the saints. Yet, she knew that Sylvia's pain was too raw for such an argument. Without having walked in her friend's shoes, Priscilla didn't want to upset her any more than she already was.

Chapter Four

It was almost a week later when Priscilla heard the news. A message had been left on the telephone in the shanty near the road, the telephone that was shared with the neighbors across that lane.

Amos Hostetler was the one who knocked on the kitchen door with the message that he had retrieved from the answering machine. He apologized to Priscilla when she answered the door, and then shared the news. It was about Sylvia, taken to bed on doctor's orders due to the stress on her heart. She had fainted while helping in the garden at her *aendi's* house. Word had spread quickly about Sylvia's illness, which seemed to be getting worse by the day. And Polly had called to make certain Priscilla knew as well.

Without a moment's delay, Priscilla went out to the barn and informed her husband about Sylvia's condition.

"I'll take you there," Stephen immediately replied. "Just give me a minute to harness the horse."

She followed him to the horse barn, and then sat on a hay bale while he opened the stall door and reached for the horse's halter to lead her outside to the main area of the building. He tied the horse to the crossties and reached for a currycomb. He glanced up, his hat tilted back on his head as he curried down his mare. Priscilla watched, proud of the care that Stephen took with the horse but also wishing that he would hurry. She was anxious to get to Polly's house so that she could find out exactly what had happened to her friend.

Stephen lifted up his hand and rested it on the horse's

withers as he looked at his wife. "You step aside, Priscilla. I don't want you getting hurt, now," he said, his voice low and soft.

She did as he instructed. Moving away from the hay bale, she leaned against the open doorway and watched as he led the horse toward the buggy. She liked to see him working with the horse. First, he slipped the harness saddle over the back of the horse, resting it just behind the withers and making certain that the girth was secure so that it wouldn't slip while supporting the shafts of the carriage. He ran his hand along the side of the horse as he moved toward the tail, a kind and calming gesture showing how much he cared for his horse.

He gently slapped her hindquarters before attaching the crupper, a V-shaped piece of black leather that latched over the tail. Once in place, Stephen buckled it at the dock in order to prevent the harness from sliding forward.

Satisfied that it was secured, he walked toward the front of the horse. In one fluid movement, he slipped over the mare's head the breast collar, a wide piece of padded leather with two long tugs that would attach to the buggy to allow for pulling and steering it.

Crossing the leather tugs over the back of the horse, Stephen moved to the buggy. Effortlessly, he pulled the buggy towards the horse, pulling it by one of the front wheels, careful to position the long, black shafts into their holders, one side at a time. When the shafts were in place, he clipped the holdback straps to the breeching before uncrossing the tugs and securing them to the swiveling base; these, in addition to the hydraulic brakes the buggy was equipped with would prevent the front fender from hitting the horse's hocks in a downhill incline or should the rig come to a sudden stop

Priscilla admired how patient, yet efficient Stephen was with the horse, speaking softly in *Deitsch* to the animal and pausing to reassure it with a loving touch on the poll and behind the ears, tugging at them playfully, before he slid the bridle with its blinders over the horse's head. He paused to make certain that the driving bit was properly and comfortably positioned in the horse's mouth, over its tongue.

In less than three minutes, Stephen had harnessed the mare and connected her to the buggy. She had enjoyed watching him work. Besides the fact that, indeed, he worked swiftly, there was a gentleness to how he handled the horse, something evident in the calm way with which the mare had responded to his touch.

"Ready?" he asked as he led the horse outside and waited for Priscilla to climb onto the step in order to get inside the buggy.

She was silent during the ride, thinking back to the church service when Sylvia looked so unwell. She had prayed for her friend, asking God to heal Sylvia, to remove the hurt and the pain. No one deserved to be treated so poorly, that was for sure and certain. But, Sylvia deserved it even less than anyone else. She was such a kind-hearted creature with soulful eyes and a godly heart. Her faith in God and people were second to none. It was horrible to think that someone was targeting her, of all people, with such bullying.

When Stephen pulled up to Polly's farm, the place where Sylvia was staying, he reached out and touched Priscilla's hand. "Be strong," he said to her.

With a nod, Priscilla climbed down from the buggy and reached inside for a loaf of the fresh bread she had baked just that morning and brought to her friend. *"Danke*, Stephen," she replied. "What time shall I expect you back?"

"I reckon an hour and a half or so. Going to run a few errands then I'll be back for you."

She watched as he slapped the reins on the horse's back and listened as he clicked his tongue. The buggy lurched forward and rolled down the driveway, back toward the road. Within a minute, it was out of sight but she could still hear the hum of the wheels and gentle clip-clop of the horse's hooves on the macadam as her husband drove away.

Inside the house, Priscilla was not surprised to see Sarah sitting at the kitchen table next to Polly.

"Wie gehts?" she asked as she sat down at the table next to her friends. "Is she doing better now?"

Polly clucked her tongue and shook her head. "Poor thing is just beside herself."

"I'm starting to think that Sylvia should air all of this," Sarah added, a dark and angry look on her face. "Make it known. Mayhaps then that Susie Byler will stop."

Priscilla frowned, remembering the promise that she had made to her friend at the church service. Sylvia didn't want people to know, and certainly not the bishop. She had been most adamant about that. Yet, clearly harboring the secret about receiving such wicked letters was causing Sylvia undue stress and, as a result, was making her physically ill.

"I've never heard of such a situation," Priscilla said softly. "I don't even know what to tell her to do."

"Never saw this coming," Polly added. "First you, then us and now Sylvia!"

"She's going after Sylvia in a much worse way," Sarah

said but, when she caught sight of Priscilla's raised eyebrow, added, "Well, almost."

"Mayhaps more personal," Priscilla said softly. "But no point in comparing. I just want it to end."

The room was dark and Sylvia looked small and meek as she lay under her bed covers. Priscilla sat on the edge of the bed and held her hand, hating how hot it felt. Fever? From high blood pressure?

"It's a virus," she whispered to Priscilla, reaching out to clutch her friend's hand. "The stress weakened my immune system and now I've caught a virus."

"Oh Sylvia," Priscilla said. "I've been praying for you since I heard the news. I pray that God gives you the strength to recover quickly and make things right again."

Sylvia nodded. "It needs to stop." Her voice was hoarse and full of sorrow. Her eyes were deep set and she had deep circles underneath them.

Priscilla didn't know what to tell her. She simply had no advice. After all, bullying among the Amish was something that she had never heard of before that first incident with Susie over her own tomatoes a few seasons back. Now, with Susie living away from her family and working among the *Englische,* there truly wasn't much that anyone could do. Not without involving Englische law and *that* was something that the Amish simply would not do.

"Just don't open the letters," Priscilla offered. She knew that did not seem like sage advice but it was all that she could offer Sylvia. "Forget about them and burn them. Tell your *aendi* about them so that she can destroy them even before you see them."

"The last one," Sylvia said, trying to sit up in the bed and ignoring Priscilla's advice. "She told me I'm not a good Christian. Told me that I should end my life, let God take me right now while there was still a chance of going to Heaven."

It took a moment for the words to register in Priscilla's mind. Not a good Christian? End her life? Did Susie truly want Sylvia to kill herself? The thought was so morbid and so disgusting to Priscilla that, for a moment, she thought that Sylvia was not thinking clearly. *Perhaps,* she ventured to consider, *she is making this up...imagining it!*

In seeing the hesitation in her friend's eyes, Sylvia sighed and reached for something in the drawer of her nightstand. It was a folded piece of paper tucked in an envelope and addressed to Sylvia. Reluctantly, Sylvia handed it to Priscilla.

After taking the note, Priscilla unfolded it. With one last glance at Sylvia's pale face and drawn expression, she turned her attention to the note. It was written at first with flowery handwriting that, after the few first words, grew sloppier and more horrid. Quickly, Priscilla's eyes scanned the words and saw the truth: Whoever was writing these letters was bullying Sylvia, attacking an innocent woman for no apparent reason.

Sylvia,

You are a worthless creature. Your illness is from the devil. The devil is calling you home. You should end it all now for even God doesn't love you.

An Amish Friend

Clutching the paper in her hand, Priscilla tried to digest

what she was reading. *Worthless! End it all now! Even God didn't love you!* She had never heard such vile words, so malicious and so full of intent to harm. Truly, no godly person could write such horrid words, full of venom and hatred.

And to have received this? Priscilla could barely imagine how Sylvia felt. She strived so hard to be a God-loving woman. They all did. They lived their lives with one purpose in mind: to honor God. To be told that even God didn't love her? Priscilla shuddered at the thought. Truly, such harsh words must have broken Sylvia's heart and damaged her soul.

With a deep breath, Priscilla shook her head and handed the note back to her friend. She met Sylvia's eyes and pleaded with her. "I...I think you really need to speak to the police," Priscilla dared to whisper. "This is dangerous. I think she really means you harm."

Sylvia took the paper back and quickly folded it again. "Nee!" She slipped the piece of paper back into the nightstand. "We don't involve the legal authorities, Priscilla. You know that."

"I dare say that this is a bit different," Priscilla countered. "She's trying to entice you to take your own life! You need to speak to someone for advice, Sylvia. If this is, indeed, Susie Byler, she is very, very sick and needs help." *Help*, Priscilla pondered. Could anything or anyone help an individual with such an unchristian mind? "Preferably before she hurts you."

Sylvia pressed her lips together, a stern expression on her face. Clearly, she was intent on not sharing this news with anyone besides Priscilla. "You say nothing to anyone, Priscilla," she warned, wagging her finger at her friend. "No talking to the bishop or discussing this with anyone. I'm going to handle this myself when I'm better."

"I don't think that's such a good idea," Priscilla replied, a drawn out tone to her voice. "She's dangerous."

Reaching out for Priscilla's hand, Sylvia stared at her friend. Her eyes pleaded for understanding and she clutched her hand, holding it until Priscilla looked at her. "Just promise me," she said. "*Bitte?*"

Reluctantly, Priscilla nodded her head in agreement. While she didn't think it was the right thing to do, she knew that this was Sylvia's fight at this point. Since Susie was not targeting her, Priscilla knew that it was not her place to interfere. If her friend didn't ask for her help, Priscilla knew better than to force it on her.

It was during the buggy ride back to their farm when Priscilla was able to reflect on her conversation with Sylvia. She waited a few minutes before sharing the details with Stephen who sat beside her, his hands tightly clutching the reins and the muscles in his jaw tensing with each word that passed through his wife's lips. Clearly, he was angry.

"Stephen?" She reached out and touched his arm. He hadn't responded to anything that she had said and that worried her.

He shook his head and glanced at his wife. "I would not believe it coming from anybody else," he finally said. "But I know you speak the truth. I find it most incredible and not in a good way."

"Ja," Priscilla agreed. "I just wish she wouldn't open those letters. Throw them out. Don't give Susie that power."

"If it is, indeed, Susie..."

Priscilla frowned. Could it be possible that it were someone else? It didn't seem likely. Not after everything that Susie had done to Priscilla and even Stephen. Then, to have targeted Polly and Sarah? But it dawned on Priscilla that none of them had reacted, not the way that Sylvia did. Indeed, by reacting in such a way, so visibly shaken and now physically ill, Sylvia was feeding the flame that kept Susie going with her bullying.

"I don't think that's likely," Priscilla responded. "Who else could do such evil things?"

Stephen sighed. "I reckon you might be right," he admitted.

Still, Priscilla admired his ability to actually give Susie the benefit of the doubt. It was admirable that his character did not jump to conclusions without analyzing all of the different angles to the situation. Just one more reason why she was so pleased with her husband and hoped that she could rise to the same level over time. For now, however, she would focus on praying for Sylvia's recovery from the stress that caused her physical harm and Susie's desperate need for help in order to repair her torn soul.

Chapter Five

Stephen waited by the buggy as Priscilla hurried out of the house. She carried a basket over her arm, which was partially hidden by the edge of her black wool shawl. It was a rainy Saturday afternoon, the air cooler than usual for April. They were going visiting with the Fischer's and would have an early supper before they had to return to their own farm for the evening milking.

He smiled as he held out his hand to assist her with stepping onto the black oval metal step in order to climb inside of the buggy.

"*Danke,*" she said as she settled into the buggy. Putting the basket on the floor by her feet, she moved over to make room for her husband.

The ride to the Fischer farm took less than fifteen minutes. Priscilla listened to the gentle rhythm of the horse's hooves and felt the light rolling of the buggy at its wheels hummed against the road. She was thankful that Stephen had left the front windows latched shut so that the hair from the horse's tail didn't fly into the front. It always tickled her throat and seemed that she couldn't get these hairs out of her nose. Yet, in the hot summer months, they had no choice but to open those windows. The buggies needed the air circulation.

When they pulled into Steve Fischer's farm, Priscilla was pleased to see another familiar buggy at the hitching rail: Gid's. If Gid were there, certainly Sarah would be, too.

The farm was smaller than Stephen's and it was clear that it needed a lot of work. The house was large but Stephen had warned her that Steve and Mimi lived in the back grossdaadihaus as there were tenants living in the main part of the house. Steve Fischer had not wanted to force them to leave when he was first married the previous autumn so he had moved his new bride into the smaller section of the house. Stephen had hinted that there had been some issues between Steve and Mimi over this, so it would be best to avoid the subject.

Despite the overcast skies and an occasional quick drizzle, the group was able to enjoy their leisure time outside at the picnic table. While the men wandered over to the barn to inspect the new milking equipment Steve had just installed, the women set about heating up the food and then brought it outside. The table was set with a simple pale blue tablecloth and a mix-match of place settings.

When the men returned to the table, everything looked like a perfect spring day. There was even a break in the clouds and a few rays of sun were finally peeking through. Priscilla was surprised that it might actually turn into a beautiful afternoon, one that was spent with friends instead of family.

And that was when the conversation had changed.

"Have you heard the latest about that Susie Byler, then?"

Priscilla caught her breath. She hadn't expected anything to be said about Susie on this day. She had no reason to, since the Fischer's lived in a neighboring church district. With grave misgivings about where the conversation was headed, she glanced at Stephen who merely lifted an eyebrow in response to his friend's question

"I heard that she's working in that gift store next to Zimmerman's Market in town," Mimi offered. "Can you imagine?" She shook her head, clearly disapproving of the situation. "What on earth was she thinking?"

Mimi's husband, Steve, reached for another piece of fried chicken and glanced at his wife. "I reckon she's thinking she needs to take care of herself now that she's been denied baptism. Might not be such a bad thing, working in a gift store. Will keep her busy, that's for sure."

"And out of trouble, I hope," Sarah added. "She's been relentless with Sylvia these past few weeks."

Sarah's brother, Gid, straightened his back and clenched his jaw. A dark shadow seemed to cover his face. "She's still at that? Bothering you girls?"

Ignoring Gid's question, Sarah hesitated before turning toward Mimi. "Where did you hear that, Mimi? About her working at that store?"

Under the table, Stephen reached for Priscilla's hand. He squeezed it gently, encouraging her to remain silent. Priscilla was all too happy to oblige. This conversation was bordering on gossip and that did not sit well with her.

"Why, that Naomi Miller! She stopped by my *daed's* store the other day when I was visiting. She was all too happy to share her updates," Mimi added lightly.

Steve groaned and shook his head. "Mimi," he said. "Enough about that Byler girl."

Sarah fluttered her hand at Steve dismissively as she leaned forward toward Mimi and Priscilla. "I don't see a 'happy ever after' in that girl's future," she whispered.

"Naomi was right quick to tell me that Susie is living in an Englische trailer. She moved out from her parents' farm, you know, and rented it. Her mamm isn't doing too well," Mimi added. "Still drinking, despite the bishop putting the ban on her. Seems her parents blamed her for all their troubles and Susie just got up and left."

Sarah scoffed. "That Naomi Miller! What a two-faced gal that one is! She was the first one to jump on the bullying bandwagon when it started; even said some right horrid things about our Priscilla here. Then, when things went rough, claimed that she had never done a thing. She's one to keep the conversation going! Not one ounce better than that crazy woman."

Covering her ears, Priscilla started to stand up. The abruptness of her action caused everyone to turn to look at her. "I can't hear one more word about this woman," she said sharply. "Right or wrong, it's just gossip and that does no one any good!"

Frustrated, she reached for Stephen's plate, getting ready to clear the picnic table. She needed to busy herself, to distance herself from the talk. The mention of Naomi Miller was just too much. How could someone who professed to be such a staunch supporter of Susie Byler during the days of bullying suddenly turn around and start spreading gossip about her own friend? It was most unchristian and Priscilla wanted nothing to do with it.

Gathering up the other empty plates, she tried to calm herself down and forced an embarrassed smile on her lips. "It's turned into such a nice day and we don't often have free time to visit. I think we should just focus on something else, something more pleasant."

Sarah frowned. "It's not gossip if it's true," she said sharply. "And after what she has done to Sylvia, why..." She paused, ignoring the sharp look from her brother. "It's just horrid, those letters!"

Steve Fischer raised both of his hands in the air. "I agree with Priscilla. Enough of this talk. I dare say the bishop wouldn't care for it. I reckon it goes against one of the ten commandants, even if it is about that Byler girl!"

"Love thy neighbor," Stephen chimed in.

"Well," Sarah said. "I can applaud the request to change subjects but I doubt I'll be sending much *lieb* in that direction!"

Despite the sharpness of her tone, the others laughed...everyone except Priscilla and Stephen. They shared a glance; an unspoken look of *knowing* that could only be shared among married couples. Priscilla dipped her head and set back to the task at hand: clearing the table and washing the dishes. *Busy hands*, she thought, *are better than busy mouths.*

For the rest of the afternoon, the three women played Scrabble while the men drank coffee and talked. The Fischers' lived in the smaller end of the farm house, the *grossdaadihaus* where the grandparents usually lived. Although Steve owned the farm, he had tenants that had lived there for years. When he had gotten married the previous fall, he hadn't felt it was proper to ask them to leave until they were properly situated and prepared to do so. Instead, he had fixed up the grossdaadihaus for his wife.

It was small but pleasant with new flooring and cabinets. Mimi certainly kept a tidy home, that was one thing that Priscilla noticed right away. And she certainly seemed happy enough, with her eyes sparkling and offering a quick laugh when the conversation warranted it. Priscilla had always liked Mimi, although she didn't always get much opportunity to visit with her.

It was on the ride home, the sun starting to dip in the sky, that she finally had a chance to talk with Stephen about the conversation. She had tried her best to have a good time but the way that the discussion had turned toward Susie had put a damper on her spirits. Gossip was not godly and she felt sinful for having even listened to it.

"Why do you think that so many people like to talk about that woman?" she asked, her hands folded on her lap as she stared straight ahead.

Stephen shrugged. "I suppose her behavior is rather shocking. No one knows what she will do next and there might be some curiosity about it, I reckon."

"I would almost feel sorry for her," Priscilla continued. "Except for how horrid those letters to Sylvia were and how she tried to claim I wrote them."

"And the false accusations and that letter to The Budget and that fake restraining order," he added, his tone terse and strained. She had never seen him look so serious and stern. "There should be no feeling sorry for her, my *fraa*. She has reaped what she has sown."

But Priscilla wasn't so certain.

Forgiveness, Priscilla told herself. That is what God would want: forgiveness for a woman who had clearly lost her way from the path of goodness and delighted in projecting her own imperfections and weaknesses onto others. By calling Sylvia a fake Christian, she was truly talking about herself. By trying to plant the seed of doubt that God loved Sylvia, Susie Byler was clearly indicating that she doubted her own goodness. By enticing Sylvia to kill herself, Susie was crying out that it was she who wanted to end it all.

The problem was, Priscilla realized, that she wasn't certain she could quite offer that type of forgiveness to a woman who had delighted so heavily in inflicting stress, pain, and suffering on so many people. Could God really expect forgiveness to come easily to such a wretched person?

Chapter Six

Priscilla glanced at the sky, apprehensive of the dark clouds rolling in as she quickly plucked the clothes pins from the line, releasing the dresses to fold and set atop the basket. In the morning, it had been sunny and bright outside, not a cloud in the sky. Nothing indicated that storms were going to roll in. Yet, there they were: black clouds forming on the horizon and slowly crawling higher in the sky, almost ready to block out the sun. Rain, indeed, was on its way.

She glanced toward the field and saw that Stephen was beginning to bring in their team of Belgians. With a good thunderstorm inevitable, Priscilla was looking forward to spending the afternoon with her husband. She pulled the rest of the laundry down from the line, folding each item as she did. Then, carrying the basket inside the house, she set it down on the floor to hurry and prepare a pitcher of fresh meadow tea for her husband.

"Going to rain some," he said as he walked in, setting his hat on the table. "Right *gut* for the crops, so can't say I'm displeased." He pulled out the chair at the head of the table and sat down; smiling his appreciation at the glass of fragrant cool tea she had just placed before him. "You feeling alright, then?" he asked, eyeballing her as she pushed at a stray strand of hair that had sprung free from her bun.

"It's muggy out," she complained.

"That it is," he concurred. "Have you seen your garden? Everything is growing like mad! Gut soil."

She nodded and sat down next to him. Resting her head

against her hand, she leaned forward and shut her eyes. "Needs weeding. Thought I might do it this afternoon, but not if it's raining."

Stephen set down his glass and stared at Priscilla. There was a gleam in his eye but he said nothing. Instead, he reached out and touched her hand. "Sure do look tired there, Priscilla," he said softly. "Mayhaps you should take a short nap."

She laughed and looked at him. A nap? "During the day?" Whoever heard of such a thing? "Stephen, I'm just fine," she scoffed, touched by his concern but also embarrassed that he would think she was so tired. "It's just the heat from the storm approaching, that's all. Plus I did laundry this morning. You know that the sheets and towel tucker me out."

He tried to hide his smile. "Tucker you out alright," he teased. He lifted the glass to his lips and finished the tea. "Um mmm. You sure do make the best meadow tea that I've ever tasted!"

She stood up. "No better than anyone else's, I reckon," she replied modestly as she plucked the pitcher off of the counter and refilled his glass. "But I'm sure glad you like it."

He reached for her hand and pulled her toward him, wrapping his arms around her waist. She bit her lower lip as she set down the pitcher on the table before turning to put her arms around his neck. "Like it I do," he whispered and started to pull her down onto his lap. "And I look forward to many, many long years of enjoying it."

She tried to fight his hold but finally gave up and let his arm pull her tight. "Stephen," she said, glancing up at the clock on the wall. Her eyes drifted to the window, quickly observing that it was becoming increasingly dark in the sky. There would be no work in the fields for a while, that was for sure and certain. Turning her attention back to her husband, she stumbled over her words. "I...I..." She didn't know what to say as the color flooded to her cheeks.

He started to nuzzle at her neck, his hands caressing her back ever so gently.

"I hear something," she whispered, squiggling to free herself from his embrace.

Stephen shut his eyes and exhaled deeply. "Who might that be?" he mumbled. Standing up, he glanced over her shoulder toward the window. Someone had definitely just pulled down the lane to their house for he saw a horse and buggy standing at the hitching post, next to the barn. He sighed and looked down at his wife. With a regretful smile, he leaned down and planted a soft, tender kiss on her lips. "Go rest, sleepy head. It's a rainy afternoon anyway and mayhaps I'll join you in a spell. Rainy spring days are perfect for a little respite from work anyhow."

Without another word, he started toward the door, pausing for just a moment to grab his hat. Priscilla leaned against the table, her knees feeling weak from the power that her husband had over her. She could feel her heart pounding and her lips still tingled from his kiss. With a soft smile, she lifted her fingers to her mouth and touched where he had just kissed her.

Humming to herself, she carried the pitcher back over to the refrigerator and began to tackle her afternoon chores.

It wasn't until later that she found out who had visited. Gid had swung by to have a private word with Stephen in the barn. With the grey sky and the dampness that seemed to clog the air, Priscilla had taken Stephen's advice and laid down for a short spell. To her surprise, she awoke almost two hours later.

Swinging her legs over the side of the mattress, she rubbed at her eyes and straightened the burgundy fabric of her dress. She had fallen asleep with her prayer kapp still on her head but it had shifted to the side. Suppressing a yawn, she stood up and shuffled to the small mirror over the dresser in order to fix her kapp.

"I don't know why I'm so tired," she said, mostly to herself as she walked out of the bedroom and into the kitchen. To her surprise, Stephen was not there. She glanced around, wondering where he could have gone. After all, she knew that the rainy weather would bring him inside for the rest of the day until it was time for evening chores.

But the room was empty.

She looked up toward the window over the sink. The yard was empty. Whoever had visited earlier had gone and taken Stephen with him. A frown creased her brow but she tried to push the feeling of dread out of her mind. Yet, despite busying herself, she knew that something was not quite right. Stephen would never leave without telling her...unless he didn't want her to know where he was going or why.

Still, his grey-topped black buggy was missing from the place where he always parked it: the side of the barn closer to the house. He was gone, indeed.

The rain had stopped when he finally returned, almost an hour after she had awaken. She was busy baking fresh bread and a peach pie from homemade canned peaches that her mamm had given to her. The kitchen smelled of warm dough and sweet peaches. He walked in, setting his hat on the counter and smacking his lips

"Um um," he said. "Something sure smells right *gut*! I sure hope that's for my supper!"

She looked up from the oven where she was bent over, using two potholders to remove the bread. The top of the loaf was crusted a golden brown, just perfect and exactly the way she liked to serve it. Setting it on the cooling rake, Priscilla leaned down and shut the over door as the pie needed a little more time cooking in the oven.

"I was surprised to see you gone when I woke up," she said lightly.

"Ah," he started, his eyes sparkling. "You took that nap after all, ja?"

Her cheeks flushed pink.

"Mayhaps a bit of coffee, then? I might be able to tell you where I disappeared too," he said teasingly. "But not before I get a little warm coffee to shake off the rain. I'm right chilled to the bone!"

Her curiosity was piqued but she asked no questions. She knew that Stephen would tell her in his own time and, from the looks of the gleam in his eye, she suspected that it was some story. It only took her a few minutes to get the water boiling on the propane stove and, by that time, Stephen was already reading *Die Botschaft*, the weekly newspaper for the Amish community. She could hear the crinkling of the newspaper as he turned the pages. The noise sounded loud in the silence of the kitchen.

When the coffee was finally ready, she set the cup in front of Stephen and sat down on the bench beside him.

He folded the paper neatly and pushed it to the center of

the table. With a dramatic hesitation, he reached for the coffee mug and lifted it to his lips. Patiently, Priscilla waited, smiling on the inside at his little game.

"Ah," he said, smacking his lips. "You do make one great cup of coffee, *fraa*."

She said nothing but watched him, curious as to what he was so anxious to tell her.

"*Vell*," he finally said, looking her directly in the eye. "It appears that we are going to have a visitor this weekend."

"A visitor?" That was news, indeed. Apart from their families and her friends, it was usually Stephen and Priscilla who did the visiting at other people's farms. That was just the way that it was done.

He nodded his head. "*Ja*, a very interesting visitor."

"Who might this 'visitor' be, Stephen?"

"Why, Bishop Miller, from a neighboring church district," he said as if anticipating a reaction from his wife. When none came, he added, "From near Strasburg."

She shrugged her shoulders. "I dare say that I don't know him. Should I?"

"Mayhaps not," Stephen admitted. "But there is a person who does know him and that would be Susie Byler."

Priscilla gasped. "What is this about, Stephen?"

He smiled and shook his head. "I wouldn't have believed it if I hadn't gone myself. But Gid stopped by, smoke coming out of his ears."

Now Priscilla was confused. Unless she was imagining things, Stephen had jumped from Susie Byler to Sarah's brother, Gid. She failed to see the connection. It was clear that, with the exception of Stephen, Susie tended to target other women, not men. Certainly there was no conflict that involved Gid. "I think you best start from the beginning," she said. "None of this is making sense."

"Seems your little friend..."

"She's not my friend," Priscilla quickly interrupted.

He laughed and held up his hand. "Hear me out," he said. "Your little friend got herself into a bit of trouble."

More trouble? Priscilla braced herself for whatever was coming next. "What type of trouble?"

"Vell," Stephen started. "She has been courting an Amish man from the Strasburg district. A John Morgan, I believe his name is. He's an older farmer with a pig farm just north of Strasburg."

"A pig farm?" Priscilla said, wrinkling her nose. If there was one thing she always knew, pig farms carried a smell with them that never left the pig farmer's skin.

Stephen nodded. "Ja. He's a bit older, never been married, and he approached her. Consequently, she visited the bishop of that *g'may*, requesting permission to take the spring baptism there. Gid's cousin lives in that district and his father-in-law is the bishop. Word trickled back to Gid. He was furious."

"Whatever on earth for?" She couldn't make any connection between Gid and Susie Byler. "Why would Gid concern himself with something like that?"

Stephen shook his head at her, smiling. "There are many things that are right in front of you, my *fraa*, but that you don't always see," he teased.

She lifted an eyebrow at his words but did not reply.

"Gid knows all about what she has done to you," Stephen explained. "And also to Sylvia."

Something clicked inside of her head. She opened her eyes wide and looked at her husband. How had she not seen this? How had she not noticed how agitated Gid had become at every discussion about Susie bothering Sylvia? How had she not made the connection between Sylvia's frequent visits from Holmes County, Ohio? While the Amish grapevine had whispered about Gid's interest in Polly's cousin long before she had returned to Ephrata for another extended visit with her Pennsylvania-based family, Priscilla hadn't paid much attention to it, presuming it was simply gossip. Now, however, the fact that they were special friends was suddenly becoming clear to Priscilla.

"Oh," she whispered. "I think I understand."

"Ja," Stephen nodded. "That's right. So Gid went right to that bishop and told him everything that had been done. Everything that Susie Byler did to you and to Sylvia. Even about those phone calls to the various farms in the district."

"Oh help!" Priscilla said, tossing her hands in the air. "That won't help one bit! Sylvia didn't want the bishop's involved!"

Stephen leaned forward. "Here's the thing, Priscilla. The bishop confronted Susie with this information and demanded a confession to the church before he would permit her to take the instructional."

Her jaw dropped open and she could barely think of one word to say.

"He asked her if she apologized to you and..." Stephen paused.

"And what?" Priscilla couldn't imagine what he would say next. There could be nothing to follow for she hadn't seen Susie since her tormentor had been refused permission to attend the instructional, not counting the day that she had caught sight of her outside of that store.

"Well," Stephen said slowly. "She said *yes*."

Priscilla felt the wind rush from her lungs. She could barely believe what she had just heard. How had Stephen learned about all of this? How had he heard this horrible story, just one more continuation of a long string of lies that seemed to simply pour out of Susie's mouth?

"I am almost inclined to say that you are making this up!" she finally gasped.

"Now, Priscilla," he said, leveling his gaze at her. "You know I'd no sooner swear than lie to you or anyone else."

Priscilla averted her eyes.

"But it does sound far-fetched, ja?" he added to soften his reprimand. "Gid denied that ever happened and the bishop wants to hear the words from your own mouth. He wants to ask you the question, Priscilla, about whether or not Susie asked for your forgiveness and repented."

"Me?" Her voice squeaked out the word and she stared at her husband. She didn't like the sound of this at all. Her life had settled down. She was so happy with Stephen, with her daily routine and with their future. She didn't want anything mired by that Susie Byler. It had been a long time since Susie had darkened her doorstep and made all of those false accusations.

And then she remembered Sylvia's letters, the ones that Susie had signed with her own name. She felt a flutter in her chest and a moment of renewed anger.

"Why not speak to Sylvia?" Priscilla asked. "She is the one that Susie is tormenting now."

Stephen gave a casual shrug. "Seems Susie is denying all of that. The letter writing. There's no proof. And Sylvia refuses to talk about it."

"I don't understand that at all!" It made no sense to Priscilla. Why would Sylvia not wish to show the letters to the bishop? Why would she not want to end the bullying? And then Sylvia's words came back to her: *I will handle this myself.* For a moment, Priscilla shuddered, realizing that Sylvia meant what she had said. By remaining silent about the letters when asked directly by the bishop, she was, indeed, intending to deal with the situation directly.

Stephen shrugged. "I can't explain Sylvia's silence but I do know that the bishop wants to talk to you since Susie was denied baptism at our church because of what she did to you."

Priscilla started to stand up but Stephen reached for her wrist and held it gently. Looking down at her husband, she shook her head. "I don't like this one bit," she whispered. "Not one."

"Me, neither," Stephen admitted. "There has been naught but strife in our lives with that girl's envious eyes focused on you. But, I'm sure hopeful that this will end it. Besides," he added as he caressed the back of her hand. His eyes softened and he pulled her toward him, embracing her with his head pressed gently against her stomach. "We have each other, ain't so? We have continually proven that, together, we don't have much to concern ourselves with that woman."

Priscilla smiled to herself. Leave it to Stephen to point

out the obvious. Despite the turmoil and emotional upheaval, their lives were set and steady. They had their faith in God, support of the community, and love for each other. With so much going for them, they truly had very little to worry about in regards to anything that had to do with Susie. She had created her own problems and alienated herself by projecting her own inadequacies onto others. *Nee*, Priscilla thought, with Stephen by her side, she had nothing to concern herself with in regard to that woman at all.

Chapter Seven

It was Friday at eleven when the black topped buggy pulled into the driveway. Priscilla was busy making cheese and the kitchen had an appealing smell to it of warm curds that were wrapped in cheese cloth and dripping over the sink. She was just about to break down the curds and salt them before putting them into the plastic cheese mold when she heard the horse and buggy coming up the driveway.

Glancing outside, she saw Stephen emerge from the barn, his battered straw hat tilted back on his head as he lifted his hand to greet whoever had arrived. She saw her husband lean his hand against the buggy and engage in conversation with the people that were inside. When Stephen turned his head to look toward the house, she knew that the visitor was going to be coming into the house. Quickly, Priscilla looked around the kitchen. Everything was tidy and neat, just the way she liked it. She disliked visiting homes where the kitchen was messy and needed a good cleaning. Priscilla's mamm had always taught her that an organized and clean kitchen was the heart of the home.

When she looked back out the window, she was startled to see an older man step out of the buggy. With his long, grey beard and black suit, Priscilla immediately knew that this was not a social visit. Yet, she did not recognize the man.

Already that morning, she had helped Stephen with milking the cows and washed their laundry to hang it to dry in the fresh spring sun. She had even spent an hour in the garden, weeding between the rows of growing vegetables. Later that afternoon, after she had prepared dinner, she intended to help

Stephen in the fields. It had been a productive day but there was still a lot of work to be done. She hoped that the visitor wouldn't stay too long.

Priscilla took the hand towel and quickly wiped down the counter before folding the cloth and hanging it over the edge of the sink. She straightened her apron and started to walk toward the door off of the kitchen in order to step outside and onto the porch. The cool spring breeze touched her skin and soothed her. It was warm in the kitchen, that was for sure and certain.

She lingered near the edge of the porch, watching as Stephen talked to the stranger. Twice she saw Stephen glancing toward the house. The second time, he lifted his hand to acknowledge her but also to indicate that she should stay put. Then, she saw him nod his head and gesture toward the house.

And that was when she saw her.

Susie Byler was sitting in the buggy.

For a moment, Priscilla caught her breath. Her pulse quickened and she felt physically ill. Hadn't Stephen mentioned something about speaking only to the bishop? And wasn't that supposed to happen over the weekend? She wrapped her hands around her midsection and leaned against the porch railing, apprehension rising within her in expectation of what might happen next.

What on earth was that woman doing sitting in her driveway?

Priscilla turned and retreated into the house. A thousands thoughts raced through her mind. She had prayed long and hard over what Stephen had told her, the other rainy day. She hadn't known what she was going to say to the bishop.

Now, with Susie Byler sitting there, just feet away from the sanctity of her own home, Priscilla felt that old rage return. How dare that woman lie to save herself? After everything that she has done? After everything she continued to do?

When she heard the footsteps on the porch, Priscilla felt faint. She placed a hand on the counter and braced herself, hoping against hope that it was the bishop and Stephen, not that woman, who would walk through that door.

The door creaked and she heard the shuffling of feet in the washroom. And then they were standing there, the three of them, staring at her.

For a moment, Priscilla couldn't believe her eyes. She had caught a glimpse of Susie outside of that gift store in town the other day but only a glimpse. Now that she was standing before her, in her own kitchen nonetheless, Priscilla was stunned with what she saw.

Gone was the pretty blond Amish woman who had tried so hard to capture the attention of Stephen Esh. Instead, she was replaced by what seemed like a woman who had been living a hard life for the past year. Her hair was still blond but the texture of straw. Priscilla knew immediately that she must have used Englische coloring on it for it was dry and brittle, even from underneath the prayer kapp.

And she was puffy in the face, a look that Priscilla remembered all too well from Susie's mamm: the look of a drinker with sunken eyes and swollen cheeks. She had also gained weight. A lot of it. Priscilla wouldn't have been surprised if the chunky yet somehow attractive young Susie Byler from yesteryear now weighed twice what she had weighed then. The woman's appearance was shocking to

Priscilla. She could scarce believe the change.

"Priscilla," Stephen started slowly. "This is Bishop Miller and I'm sure you remember Susie Byler."

Priscilla smiled at Bishop Miller but made no acknowledgement of Susie's presence.

The bishop removed his hat and took a step forward. There was a strained look about him and Priscilla immediately realized that this situation was just as troublesome to others as it was to her. "Priscilla," he started. "Stephen told me that he has informed you of the reason why I am here before you with Susie Byler."

Despite not wanting to, Priscilla caught herself glancing at Susie when the bishop mentioned her name. Swallowing, Priscilla nodded. "*Ja,* he did that."

The bishop took a deep breath. "*Vell,* as you know, baptism is a very serious matter and, when Susie came to me to attend the instructional, it was brought to my attention that there were some transgressions from her past that had hindered her baptism into her own church district."

Priscilla caught a glowering look tossed her way from Susie's direction. She ignored it, feeling a wave of anger washing over her. She did not want that woman in her house. She felt dirty and soiled just for having that horrid woman who had caused her and her friends so much trouble and pain standing in her kitchen. Yet, a quick look over at Stephen, she realized that she was not going through this alone. He was there to support her.

"Now," the bishop continued. "I cannot grant any approval for baptism instructional until this matter is cleared up. I have spoken to some length to Susie regarding what transpired. I have also spoken to your bishop for his perspective on the matter. Now, I would like to hear from you, Priscilla."

The color drained from Priscilla's face and Stephen stepped forward, reaching out to hold her arm. "Easy," he mumbled. "You want to sit down, then?"

She shook her head, refusing to appear weak at this moment. "*Nee*, I'm fine," she whispered and lifted her chin. "What is it that you wish to know, Bishop?"

He cleared his throat. "It is important that I know if Susie has repented her sins against you," he said, leveling a stern look at Priscilla. "Only a person with a pure heart can be saved."

Stephen tightened his grip on Priscilla's arm and she glanced at him. What was she supposed to say? But Stephen gave her no guidance. He merely raised an eyebrow.

"I'm sure I wouldn't know whether she has a pure heart," Priscilla said slowly. "That's not something I'm capable of judging."

The bishop lifted a finger in the air. "But if she has come to you and repented, asked for forgiveness for her sins, that is an indication of seeking God."

"I see," she replied.

There was an uncomfortable silence for a long moment, Priscilla waiting for someone to speak but everyone waiting for her next words. She had none. The clock ticked on the wall and, outside, a horse drawn buggy whizzed along the road.

"Priscilla?" Stephen finally said, nudging her gently. "You need to respond."

"I...I don't think I know what the question is," she

admitted truthfully. *What was the bishop asking?*

"Has Susie Byler come to you, confessing her sins and repenting? Has she sought your forgiveness?" the bishop asked, an edge to his voice.

It would have been too easy to admit the truth, to simply shake her head and say "*nee.*" It would have been too easy to let vengeance take over and watch Susie's future be destroyed with that one simple word that negated Susie's final lie.

Yet, there was pride in doing so. Priscilla immediately thought of the clothes line and the women who hung out their dirty clothing in order to appear the hardest working woman. Pride, she thought quickly. And she realized that she had a choice to make: tell the truth or stop the bullying for once and for all.

To admit the truth and to let the world see it, she pondered, was the same as airing dirty laundry in order to make one look better than the others. Yet, deep down, those women were nothing more than prideful women who were cutting corners rather than truly working hard and being the godly and hard working women that they professed to be.

There had to be another way.

If Priscilla said that one word, "*nee*", Susie would never get to become a baptized member of the Amish church. She would never be able to marry that John Morgan; and, if that was something she truly wanted, Priscilla did not feel as though she had the right to deny Susie that potential gift of grace from God. Perhaps she had truly changed, Priscilla thought. Besides, wouldn't she betray Sylvia's wishes, no matter how strongly Priscilla disagreed with her friend's position, if she were to mention these letters? No, she came to realize: It was not her place to make that decision. If it was God's will, He and only Him would let it be known.

Lifting her chin, Priscilla turned and stared at Susie, their eyes burning into each other's. Stephen still stood by his wife's side, giving Priscilla the strength to face this woman who had been a problem for so long, a woman who had tried so hard to ruin Priscilla's reputation and then worked at destroying her relationship with Stephen, the very thing that Susie had wanted more than anything. When Susie failed, she finally attempted to discredit both of them in a very public manner. In the end, Susie's bullying had caused her to lose all of her credibility among the community.

It was a miracle that any Amish man was willing to marry her, especially now that the new church district was aware of what she had done.

"Did Susie tell *you* that she repented to me?" Priscilla heard herself asking.

The bishop frowned. "That is why we are here," he said, his impatience becoming evident. "To verify that she did."

Priscilla held Susie's gaze. She watched the reaction of the lost woman standing before her. *Who am I*, she thought, *to steal her future?* "Ja," Priscilla said. "She repented."

There was another moment of silence. Both Stephen and the bishop seemed surprised by Priscilla's announcement. But it was Susie's reaction that startled Priscilla. Her eyes narrowed and she glared at Priscilla. A slight motion caught Priscilla's attention. It was Susie's hand. She had tightened her fist as if angry and wishing she could physically harm Priscilla.

Ignoring Susie, Priscilla turned to the bishop. "If she told you that she was aware of her actions and repentant of her past behavior, I believe her. And I believe that she means it. That is all of the confession and forgiveness seeking that I need."

"But has she come to you?"

"She stands before me now," Priscilla stated, gesturing toward the woman before her. "Is that not enough? Clearly she wishes to move on and to forget the past, to focus on the future. The fact that she stands here is enough for me and I extend my own hand in forgiveness to her." With that, Priscilla held out her hand, waiting for Susie to take it.

There was a moment of hesitation, too long for Priscilla's liking. But Susie finally reached out and took Priscilla's hand, holding it limply in her own for a single, short shake.

"This ends it, then" Priscilla said firmly, staring directly into Susie's face. "Ja?"

"It ended long ago," Susie mumbled. It was clear that Susie had nothing further to say to Priscilla.

"For Sylvia's sake, I sure hope so," Priscilla whispered, her voice low so that the bishop wouldn't hear, before quickly releasing Susie's damp, clammy hand. In her mind, she heard Sylvia's meek voice while ill, professing to take care of the situation when she was well. Now, if Priscilla's acceptance of forgiveness were enough to get Susie back on track with the church and her courting friend, perhaps Susie would finally stop harassing Sylvia and focus on her own future.

The bishop seemed somewhat abated but there was a look in his eye when he turned his gaze from Priscilla to Susie. "Sisters in Christ love one another," he said. "Pray for one another and be kind toward another." Yet his eyes were staring directly at Susie. "Are these things that you can do, sister?"

Priscilla saw Susie swallow before she nodded her head, a forced nod that was stiff and unconvincing even to Priscilla. "*Ja,*" she said. "I will love my fellow sister and pray for her."

Satisfied, the bishop nodded his head and turned back to Priscilla. "Danke for your time, Priscilla." He looked at Stephen and nodded. "Our business is over here so we shall not take anymore of your time."

Stephen and Priscilla stood in the middle of the kitchen, silent for several long minutes until they heard the horse and buggy rattle down their driveway. When it was apparent that it was gone, Stephen turned to look at his wife and nodded his head once.

"Well done, my Priscilla," he said approvingly. "You have shown yourself as a true Christian and I feel humbled by the wisdom of your answer to the bishop"

There were tears in her eyes but she fought them back by blinking. "Oh Stephen," she whispered. "I so want this to end, want her to stop. Do you think that she ever will?"

He placed his hands on her shoulders and smiled down into her face. With his thumb, he wiped at the tear that threatened to fall from her one eye. "I think you have done the best that you can do to be a strong woman. You have demonstrated your character over and over again, Priscilla. She should have no more quarrels with you, not if she wants to marry this John Morgan and live among our people."

Priscilla nodded, hoping that her husband was correct. "And what of Sylvia?"

With a deep breath, Stephen nodded his head. "I do

believe that this is something she must deal with. Although," he paused. "I'd think Susie would be quite the fool to continue with her games at this point. You may have ended it for her, too." He leaned down at planted a soft kiss on her forehead. "A clever and wise woman you are, Priscilla Esh."

Yet, there was a foreboding feeling inside of Priscilla. Despite Stephen's confidence in what she had said to the bishop, she wasn't convinced that she had, indeed, seen the last of Susie Byler.

Chapter Eight

Priscilla sat on the porch chair, sipping at a glass of meadow tea while watching the sunset behind the barn. The clothes that she had washed earlier in the day hung from the clothes line. She knew that she needed to take it down but was enjoying just relaxing for a moment as the day began to wind down.

Stephen sat next to her in his own chair, a rocking chair with weathered caning in the back and chipped paint on the arms. As he rocked back and forth, the wooden rockers creaked against the porch floorboards. His eyes scanned the horizon, watching the birds dip in the sky over the fields, their evening song welcoming the approaching nightfall.

She was crocheting placemats with a fine thread. It was too warm to crochet blankets, the yarn being too thick, and she could sell the placemats to the stores that tourists frequented. Since she loved crocheting, it was something she enjoyed doing, even if she did not make a much profit in doing so.

"Stephen, I wonder about Bishop Miller and what he decided to do," she said, breaking the silence. It had been a week since the bishop had visited their farm and, despite the magnitude of the visit, they hadn't spoken about it, each very reflective of their inner thoughts about the matter. "Have you heard, then?"

Stephen stopped rocking for a moment. The silence caught her attention and she looked up from her crocheting. He was staring off into the distance but it was clear that he was not watching anything in particular. She waited patiently for him to collect his thoughts before responding.

"*Ja,*" he finally said. "I have heard something that may be of interest to you."

She set the half-finished placemat onto her lap and gave him her undivided attention. "Please tell me."

A sparrow flew by the porch and landed on the branch of a tree. For a moment, it appeared that Stephen was watching it and Priscilla glanced in that direction. It chirped a few times before taking off into flight again, heading away from the house and toward the open hayloft in the barn.

"Seems to me that the wedding with John is postponed. The bishop wants more time for Susie to go through a proving," Stephen started. "He was not impressed that she lied to him about asking for forgiveness from you. He is also questioning other things that she has said, such as denying those letters to Sylvia."

He paused and Priscilla waited, sensing that there was more. "He was, however, impressed with your willingness to forgive. That is why he is giving her another chance. Because of you."

"I see."

Stephen turned to look at her. "You did a good thing, Priscilla Esh," he said. "Forgiving that woman was a right gut thing and reminds me of what a *gut* woman you are. A *gut* wife, for sure and certain, and a gut mamm."

She laughed. "*Gut* wife, *mayhaps*, but mamm? One day, *ja?*"

Stephen raised an eyebrow and looked at her. There was a sparkle to his eye and he smiled. "One day soon, I reckon, ain't so?"

For a moment, his words lingered before them. She

frowned, not understanding what he was saying. And then it dawned on her. The feeling of being so tired. The way she felt in the mornings. The fact that she had started to gain weight.

"Oh!" she whispered.

Now it was Stephen laughing. He reached out his hand to take hers. Then, gently, he pulled her out of her chair and onto his lap. He wrapped his arms around her waist and smiled up at her. "How could you not know? I've known for a while and been waiting for you to tell me!"

The color had drained from her face and she felt overwhelmed at the realization that she was, indeed, pregnant. "I...I just didn't think about it," she whispered. "There have been so many changes that I thought I was tired from working so hard and gaining weight from my cooking!"

"And being sick in the morning?"

"I..." She was embarrassed to admit that she had thought very little about it beyond not feeling well.

He laughed again and hugged her tightly. "Oh Priscilla," he said, a satisfied tone to his voice. "What a right *gut fraa* you are, indeed!"

Giving into her husband's embrace, Priscilla closed her eyes for a few moments, her head resting gently on Stephen's left shoulder. The light evening breeze was gently caressing her face and she felt blessed to have this wonderful man, *her* Stephen, for her lifetime husband and companion.

She would give him many sons and daughters. He would raise their sons in the same righteous way he had himself been raised, teaching them how to respect and care for the land which, one day, would help provide for their own families. She would raise their daughters just the way she had been raised by her own mamm, teaching them to keep a *gut* home for the family and to respect their father for he was their provider and the person to lean on for comfort and moral support. They all would live happy lives within the *g'may*, guided by their faith in the Lord and the love He had bestowed to them.

This, Priscilla thought was their way; the way of the Amish.

At this precise moment, she was startled off her reverie by a sudden stir coming from the open window in the barn's hayloft; turning her attention to it, she marveled at the two sparrows, flying side by side, each holding a blade of hay in their beak. Landing on a forked tree branch, before resuming their flight back to the barn, both birds gently dropped their building material at the center of something round and firm; something that, even from the distance, was starting to look like a nest.

Time to start feathering my own nest, Priscilla thought as she quietly got up and started toward the clothes line, careful not to wake up Stephen from the blissful nap he had fallen into as she pulled in the laundry, quietly folding each piece as she listened to the gentle sound of the birds chirping from the tree.

Song: Pretty Good At Lying

Written by Katie G. *and Anthony Vitale*

I can listen to all your stories
Sing them to me like a song
All the details
All the glory
I don't care that they're all wrong

Chorus
You're pretty good at lying
You're pretty good at telling me you love me
I never saw it coming
You're pretty good
You're pretty good

I know there won't be a happy ever after
This good thing will come to an end
I don't let my dreams be my master
And I'm not sure if we could be friends

Chorus
You're pretty good at lying
You're pretty good at telling me you love me
I never saw it coming
You're pretty good
You're pretty good

Walking home by myself
It ain't easy
Especially on a sunny day
What hurts the most
Is bumping into each other
And you've got nothing to say

Chorus
You're pretty good at lying
You're pretty good at telling me you love me
I never saw it coming
You're pretty good
You're pretty good

You can download this song by visiting Katie G's iTunes page, which is located at: https://itunes.apple.com/us/artist/katie-g/id588926464

Book Discussion Questions

By Pamela Jarrell, Administrator of The Whoopie Pie Book Club on Facebook and author of the Whoopie Pie Pam Kitchen Collection.

1. Why do you think Susie Byler turned her attention to tormenting Sylvia?

2. What do you think of how Priscilla and the other girls handled the Susie Byler situation?

3. What was Sylvia's motive in showing Priscilla the letters but asking her to remain silent about them?

4. Why do you think Susie keeps bullying? With all that she has been through, why hasn't she stopped?

5. Why was it so important to John Morgan that he knew Susie had apologized?

6. What do you think about Priscilla's approach to extending an olive branch to Susie when confronted by the Bishop?

7. Have you ever been in a situation where you had to confront someone who said or did something that upset you?

8. The Amish practice forgiveness and avoid confrontation. In such a situation as Priscilla faces, would you be able to continue praying for Susie Byler?

Love reading Amish romances and Amish Christian fiction? Please join the Whoopie Pie Book Club Group on Facebook where members share stories, photos, book reviews, and have weekly book club discussions.

ABOUT THE AUTHOR

The Preiss family emigrated from Europe in 1705, settling in Pennsylvania as the area's first wave of Mennonite families. Sarah Price has always respected and honored her ancestors through exploration and research about her family's history and their religion. At nineteen, she befriended an Amish family and lived on their farm throughout the years. Twenty-five years later, Sarah Price splits her time between her home outside of New York City and an Amish farm in Lancaster County, PA where she retreats to reflect, write, and reconnect with her Amish friends and Mennonite family.

Find Sarah Price on Facebook and Goodreads!
Learn about upcoming books, sequels, series, and contests!

Contact the author at sarahprice.author@gmail.com.
Visit her weblog at http://sarahpriceauthor.wordpress.com or
on Facebook at www.facebook.com/fansofsarahprice.

CPSIA information can be obtained at www.ICGtesting.com
Printed in the USA
LVOW06s1504241013

358456LV00016B/828/P